# Little Explorer's Guide to
# QUEENSLAND NATIONAL PARKS

Outdoor activities and experiences for adventurous kids

**WRITTEN BY**
**CHLOE BUTTERFIELD**

**ILLUSTRATED BY**
**DEBORAH BIANCHETTO**

# TABLE OF CONTENTS

Cairns

Townsville

Mount Isa

Rockhampton

Hervey Bay

Brisbane

Gold Coast

# GIRRAWEEN
## NATIONAL PARK

Trek west to discover the land of the rock giants.
At Girraween your adventures will include boulder
hopping, creek dipping, ridge walking and up-close
wildlife encounters.

Here beyond the range, where the wildflowers
wander and the rock peaks tower tall, you'll have
endless opportunities to play and discover.

# GIRRAWEEN NATIONAL PARK
## ID CARD

**PARK ESTABLISHED:** 1966
**KNOWN FOR:** Giant boulders and rocky outcrops
**SIZE:** 113km²
**HOME OF:** Various Aboriginal groups
**GEOGRAPHY:** Eucalypt forest atop ancient granite

*LITTLE EXPLORER'S GUIDE*

## SPOTTED-TAILED QUOLL

Rustle, rustle ... what's that sound? It might be our cheeky mate the Spotted-tailed Quoll, hunting in the darkness for its next snack of mammals, birds, insects or fruit. These furry friends are the size of a cat and have pretty white spots down their back and trailing tail. Quolls have very sharp teeth and powerful jaws to catch and crush their prey.

You can help protect our quolls by slowing down on roads at night, supporting quoll research programs and asking your government to protect quoll habitat. We've found the best way to share the love is to talk about special animals, plants and places to raise awareness.

## WILDFLOWERS

Travel in autumn for your best chance to experience colourful Girraween, meaning 'place of flowers' in Aboriginal language. There are over 700 types of blooms to see, draw, photograph and count.

## DOUBLE DRUMMER CICADA

The sound of the Australian bush is often a relentless, high-pitched whining. This is the song of the male Double Drummer Cicada at Girraween. Cicadas spend almost all of their lives under the ground. They emerge to mate on the surface for a few weeks and when they die they become delicious snacks for birds, reptiles and marsupials. Everyone has their place in the cycle of bush life. You'll definitely hear the cicadas, but I wonder if you can see them too – look for clues on large eucalypts and count how many exuviae (skins) you can find.

## MARVELLOUS MACROPODS

The safe grasslands around campsites are a relaxing spot for wallabies and Eastern Grey Kangaroos to hang with their mates. A group of kangaroos is called a 'mob'. Did you know that Eastern Greys talk to each other with 'clucking' sounds and deep 'coughs'?

## BOULDERS

Take a hike on any of the main tracks at Girraween and you'll be able to experience feeling incredibly small against huge, towering rock formations. Feel the roughness and strength of the granite as you duck and weave through naturally made caves, hiding holes and rock castles!

## BELL'S TURTLE

Taking a dip in the cool waters of Girraween is pretty magical. I wonder who else is in there with you? The Bell's Turtle enjoys pools with sandy bottoms, sunny rocky outcrops and occasionally popping up to say hi. These guys only live in the New England Tablelands, so it's important to protect their habitats. Put your rubbish in the bin, stay on the tracks and try to use as little water as you can.

## GRANITE LEAF-TAILED GECKO

You'll need your keenest sight to spot these little beasties. Tiptoe around your campsite at night and scour the trunks of trees to find your new best friend. These guys love the nights in their warm, dry environment and hang out on trees and rocks with the most amazing lichen-like camouflage – they almost appear to melt away in front of your eyes.

Geckos require superpower holding strength to climb upside-down on tree trunks and rocks. To get the best grip, they've evolved special scales under their toes, each with microscopic hooks that work a bit like velcro!

# ACTIVITIES

## GOODNESS GECKOS

Draw your best leaf-tailed gecko and use adjectives to describe their features.

Imagine if you could turn into a gecko superhero.

**What crazy stuff would you do with your expert climbing powers?**

## BULGING BOULDERS

Ever noticed how you start to imagine things when you stare long enough? **Take your book on today's adventure and see how many faces in the rock you can find.**

| LOCATION | TALLY ⦀ |
|---|---|
| The Pyramid | |
| Granite Arch | |
| Bald Rock Creek | |
| Underground Creek | |
| Castle Rock | |

## RANGER'S TIPS

All explorers must follow the tracks and signs set up by the National Park Rangers.

These keep us from getting lost or hurting ourselves in isolated places and it keeps plants and animals safe from noisy, stomping people near their homes. Don't forget the scientists' code – **RESPECT FOR FLORA, FAUNA AND COUNTRY!**

Wear sturdy shoes with lots of grip for rock walks and head back to camp if the rain becomes heavy – granite is slippery when wet.

**ENJOY EXPLORERS!**

## SCAVENGER HUNT   *GO ON A SCAVENGER HUNT – HOW MANY WILDFLOWERS CAN YOU FIND?*

# Lamington
## NATIONAL PARK

Journey to an ancient land where forests are deep and creatures elusive. Where mighty cliffs grow tall and rocky above emerald sweeping valleys. The rivers here end in spectacular waterfalls, and through the mist some explorers see vibrant rainbows.

If you're lucky you'll spot the majestic Regent Bowerbird or the trailing tail of a shy and remarkable creature – the Albert's Lyrebird. Throw in some friendly furry faces from the local pademelon, the deepest greens and the tallest trees and you know you're at Lamington National Park.

## LAMINGTON NATIONAL PARK
### ID CARD

**PARK ESTABLISHED:** 1915
**KNOWN FOR:** Rainforest birds and waterfalls
**SIZE:** 220km²
**HOME OF:** Yugambeh people
**GEOGRAPHY:** Gondwana forest on steep mountain range

## FUNGI

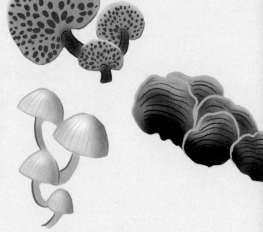

High altitude and thick forest mean rain and mist occur more often up here – perfect conditions for fungi. The forest floor and high up into the trunks of trees are littered with colourful spongy delights. There are big ones, tiny ones, fans, toadstools, types that bloom overnight, even types that glow in the dark! If you can dream it, it probably exists in nature. How many types can you find?

## RICHMOND BIRDWING

These butterfly giants float on the wind like elegant fluttering rainbows. Many years ago, Brisbane streets were filled with bursts of colour when the birdwings emerged from their chrysalises. Now one of Australia's rarest butterflies, they hide in the national park, always in search of the exact vine their pupae eat to survive. Look out for shades of green and yellow, with a distinctive red splash near the head. You can do your part by planting the Birdwing Butterfly Vine in your home or school gardens and helping to bring back our city's treasure.

## ALBERT'S LYREBIRD

Its magnificent trailing tail might be lost beneath the deep green forest, but the first time you hear its song, you'll know you're in the company of ancient greatness. The Albert's Lyrebird is the smaller and less fancy cousin of the Superb Lyrebird, but don't let its small stature and rusty-brown plumage fool you – this creature is almost as elusive as it gets. Few who travel here are lucky enough to spot the shy fellow as it half-runs, half-flies with an occasional leap to evade spies. Albert's roam within an extremely limited range and lucky Lamington happens to be a favourite spot. These lyrebirds go to all sorts of lengths to maintain their privacy, including stamping down plants to make a platform from which to perform mating dances and calling rarely like a bird and more like a dingo howling. Quiet hikers will hear them echo through the dense forest – will you be one of them?

## WATERFALLS

Ever wondered what happens to rain after it falls from the sky? At Lamington you can see the process with your own eyes. Pristine rivers at the tops of the mountain fill with cool, fresh water and hurry their way down the slopes. On their journey they bring life to the forest, watering the trees, allowing animals to drink and filtering out the 'yucky' bits. Down they go, swishing and swashing till finally they reach the edge. Here they leap into the air and dive perfectly to the pools below, letting off cool mist that glistens in the sunlight as they go. These are the majestic waterfalls of Lamington National Park, every one special and different in its own way. Remember to stay on the trails and bring a camera or a sketchbook so you never forget your first time feeling tiny against the roar of power.

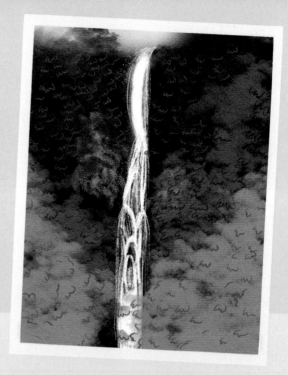

## LAMINGTON SPINY CRAYFISH

A rainy day is the best time to see these bright blue, armoured beasties wandering along tracks. These wave their large claws above their head and yell out with a 'hiss' if interrupted. Stand clear, their claws are sharp and tempers short. These crayfish need the rainforest to survive and only live in a few special places above 300m altitude. Watch closely to work out how they move around with that hard, spiny shell on.

## RED-NECKED PADEMELON

Sweet beady eyes watch you play, climb and hike the twisting trails – always listening, always noticing. Furry little pademelons spring and bounce through the undergrowth in search of late afternoon snacks of juicy grass. Even though they're wallabies, these little fellas have short tails, round bellies and a tinge of red around the neck and shoulders. To let their friends know of danger, they thump their back legs into the ground. Keep your eyes peeled for these pouched visitors on roadsides and grassy areas around dusk.

## SATIN BOWERBIRD

You can spot one of these cheeky feathered friends in many places in the park, but harder to find is their special bower, meticulously groomed and designed for attracting a female companion. These glossy black thieves shine with beauty as they roam the forest (and maybe your campground) to collect items in their favourite shade of blue to decorate their display sites. If you look down low beneath the undergrowth, you might spot one of these special bowers where the male birds have built up perfect circular walls of spindly sticks, leaving a stage in the centre for them to wait for their perfect match to notice them – blue love at first sight.

# ACTIVITIES

## SPOT THE DIFFERENCE

The best explorers have a keen eye for detail. Practice your skills and see if you can find the 10 differences between the two birdwings.

## FIND MY HABITAT MATCHUP

You'll encounter many secret habitats at Lamington National Park.
Match the animals to their habitats through the maze to help you remember who lives where.

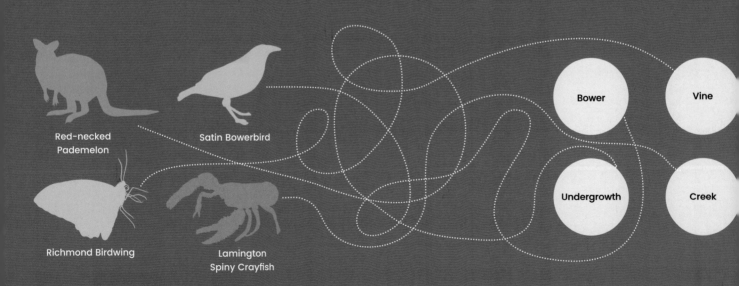

Red-necked Pademelon

Satin Bowerbird

Richmond Birdwing

Lamington Spiny Crayfish

Bower

Vine

Undergrowth

Creek

# BUNYA MOUNTAINS
## NATIONAL PARK

Take a visit to Bunya Mountains where it's colder up
high in the rich shady greens of the second-oldest
national park in Queensland. Here you can find the
world's largest group of Bunya trees and unlimited
stars in the night sky.

## BUNYA MOUNTAINS NATIONAL PARK
## ID CARD

**PARK ESTABLISHED:** 1908

**KNOWN FOR:** Bunya nuts and gathering festivals

**SIZE:** 192km$^2$

**HOME OF:** Wakka wakka, Jarowair, Djaku-nde and Barrungam people

**GEOGRAPHY:** Mountain range and cool rainforest

*LITTLE EXPLORER'S GUIDE*

## FIREFLIES

The days are fun, but the nights are magical. From October to November at dusk, head to where the grass meets the forest edge to watch these tiny flying beetles light up the darkness with their twinkling that they flash from glowing bellies to attract mates.

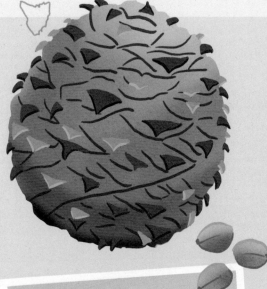

## GATHERING FOR BUNYAS

Bunya trees grow 30m or taller and from the prickly leaves and perfectly straight branches grow the most amazing giant cones. Each can weigh up to 4kg! Inside hide approximately 60 seeds that can be roasted, boiled or ground into flour.

Every three years Aboriginal people would walk hundreds of kilometres to gather and eat the nuts. This was a time for meetings and decision-making, trade, ceremonies and to share ideas. The trees are very important culturally and environmentally and each Aboriginal group was responsible for taking care of certain trees. Sadly, after colonisation, the last big gathering took place around 1902.

## RED-NECKED WALLABY

You're sure to spot many of these macropod friends on your visit. Grey, with a rusty-coloured patch around their necks; the adults feed in open grassy areas. Babies, however, get 'hidden' in the bushes close by for safety once they're out of the pouch.

## BLACK-BREASTED BUTTONQUAIL

This little round, ground bird is tricky to spot. They use excellent camouflage to hide amongst the leaf litter where they seek invertebrates and seeds. Look out for circles amongst the leaves from pivot feeding – scratching with one foot while turning around in a circle with the other, how strange!

## CHOCOLATE WATTLED BAT

Did you know that the largest colony of Chocolate Wattled Bats lives in the old schoolhouse in the Bunya Mountains? Delicious though they may sound, these funny fellas are actually named after their rich brown fur. They have tiny eyes, but HUGE ears and eat moths close to home. In the winter, when it's cold, they huddle up close with their male or female group and hibernate for the winter.

## COLLARED DELMA

No legs and slithers ... but it's not a snake! You've found the smallest legless lizard in Australia. They use their long tails to jump off the ground if threatened. Their favourite habitat is rocky outcrops and scientists think they might live under the same rock their entire life. Collared Delmas are harmless to humans, but be careful moving rocks as you might disturb their eggs.

## GREAT BARRED FROG

In the wet forests of the mountains, listen for the night call that sounds like *waaaark*. They cleverly lay their eggs in water, then kick them out to stick onto mud or rocks. Once the tadpoles are big enough, they flick out of the egg sac and safely drop into the water below.

## LOGGING HISTORY

Take a look around and focus on the largest tree you can see. Now imagine if the whole forest had trees like this.
After colonisation, European settlers removed many trees in this area. They set up 25 sawmills to cut logs and used livestock to pull them along. Eventually, groups of brave people convinced the government that logging should stop and a national park was created in its place.

# ACTIVITIES

## LIFECYCLE FUN

Order the pictures of the Great Barred Frog to show the stages of its metamorphic lifecycle.

Frog

Froglet

Eggs with tadpoles inside

Tadpole

Tiny egg mass

## RANGER'S TIPS

Your explorer boots have been on many adventures, but they can also carry soil and plant diseases that are invisible to the human eye.

Wash your boots before you arrive and at the special wash stations at the start of track entrances. Thanks for keeping the Bunyas safe.

## WHERE'S WALLABY?

Follow the maze to help the wallaby find her way back to her joey she hid in the bushes. Watch out for predators!

**NIGHT TALLY** COUNT THE FIREFLIES EACH NIGHT AND KEEP A TALLY. WHICH DAY HAD THE MOST? CAN YOU GUESS WHY?

# NOOSA
## NATIONAL PARK

Sometimes great things come in small packages.
This little park has so much to offer, from gentle streams to
rocky cliffs and not to mention those vast, sweeping views
across the bright blue Coral Sea.

Let's get sandy underfoot and come explore this pretty part
of the world.

## NOOSA NATIONAL PARK
### ID CARD

**PARK ESTABLISHED:** 1939
**KNOWN FOR:** Whale- and dolphin-spotting
**SIZE:** 30km²
**HOME OF:** Kabi Kabi people
**GEOGRAPHY:** High dunes and wallum heath

## KOALA

Don't forget to look up! Noosa is home to a small population of cuddly Koalas. You'll find them sleeping 20 hours a day nestled in the forks of Eucalypts – the only food they like to eat. Koala babies live in backwards-facing pouches when small, then hitch a ride on mum's back. As they get older they eat liquid poo called 'pap' to help them get used to the strong taste of gum leaves. Switch on all your senses for Koala clues – look for deep scratch marks on trees, avocado-shaped droppings and smell for Eucalyptus. In 2022, Koalas were declared as endangered in Queensland. You can help by reporting your sightings to the Noosa City Council.

## BURTON'S LEGLESS LIZARD

The Burton's is a 'flap footed' lizard, it has no real legs but small flaps on each side of its body. Its pointy nose is unmistakable and it can open its mouth wide to eat. Unlike snakes, legless lizards have an unforked tongue and ear openings.

## GLOSSY BLACK-COCKATOO

Sneak in quietly and listen for the munch... it might be a Glossy Black-Cockatoo snacking on the seeds of sheoaks. These hungry fellows can eat up to 580 cones a day and to help them out, the council has been buying back land with plenty of sheoak trees to make sure they stick around. Glossies are threatened and much more shy and quiet than other black-cockatoos that gather in large groups.

## COMMON FRINGE-LILY

Between August and November, enjoy counting the three-petal lilies that hide in the undergrowth. Shades of purple, blue and white with frilly edges bring a splash of colour to the bush.

## GROUND PARROT

Vulnerable in Queensland, the Ground Parrot wanders through the undergrowth with its long legs and toes, eating seeds that have fallen to the ground. These curious creatures make a bowl-shaped nest directly on the ground, hidden by plants. Ground living is not for the faint-hearted and unfortunately these shy guys have been seriously affected by habitat destruction and feral cats and foxes. Ecologists have been using special recorders to listen for their distinctive call. You have more of a chance at hearing them than seeing them. They sound like *tsee, tsee, tsee, tsit* ... even though you barely see, see, see it.

## WALLUM FROGLET

At just 2cm long, these hoppers are tiny! Look out for them when it's raining and at night. They're a type of acid frog and live near brown lakes. The lakes become acidic when leaves rot and lower the pH in the water. Wallum eggs stick together and cling onto plants underneath the water. If exploring at night, listen for a metallic *tching tching* that gets faster and faster.

## DOLPHINS

All year round this is a great spot to watch dolphin pods frolic. Scientists think that dolphins leap to communicate, and perhaps different movements mean different things. Dolphins use echolocation to socialise and work in teams. They make a sound using their melon (top of their head) and wait for it to echo back after bouncing off objects underwater.

## KEELBACK SNAKE

A special species lives here near rivers and swamps. You can find them day or night and although they are excellent swimmers and climbers, they are not venomous to humans. They use their keeled scales to grip slippery surfaces and if threatened produce a fart smell! They are especially important because they can eat Cane Toads without getting sick.

## RED GOSHAWK

Soaring above you are the rarest of all our raptors. With a wingspan of a metre and bare, scaly legs, you can tell them apart from eagles. Goshawks like waiting quietly in trees near river banks from which they dart out to catch birds, mammals, reptiles and insects. Look for nests high in the forks of trees.

# ACTIVITIES

## TRACK TRACER

Use the clues to track down which animal from Noosa National Park has been sneaking around.

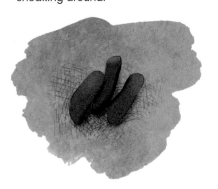

..................................

..................................

..................................

..................................

## TRUE OR FALSE

Answer the quiz below to find out the differences between snakes and lizards.

| | | |
|---|---|---|
| LIZARDS MUST HAVE LEGS | TRUE | FALSE |
| SNAKES HAVE EAR OPENINGS | TRUE | FALSE |
| SNAKES HAVE A FORKED TONGUE | TRUE | FALSE |
| SNAKES DO NOT HAVE EYELIDS | TRUE | FALSE |
| BOTH SNAKES AND LIZARDS ARE 'ECTOTHERMIC' (COLD BLOODED) | TRUE | FALSE |

## ECHOLOCATION   *INVENT YOUR OWN SECRET DOLPHIN CALL LANGUAGE WITH A FRIEND — DON'T FORGET TO WRITE DOWN HOW TO MAKE EACH SOUND!*

# K'GARI
## NATIONAL PARK

A floating tropical island teeming with incredible animals, silky white sand, lush rainforest and the freshest water in the country.

Traditional home of the Butchulla people for over 5,000 years, this is K'Gari (Fraser Island).

# K'GARI (FRASER ISLAND) GREAT SANDY NATIONAL PARK
## ID CARD

**PARK ESTABLISHED:** 1992 gained World Heritage Status
**KNOWN FOR:** Pristine freshwater lakes
**SIZE:** 1,660km$^2$
**HOME OF:** Butchulla people
**GEOGRAPHY:** Sand island

## DINGO

Clever eyes and soft feet follow you silently through the forest. Dingoes are excellent at keeping feral animals away and like to feast on fish, crabs, reptiles and marsupials for their tucker. Sometimes they even eat berries and scraps. Dingoes are fluffy and cute, but they're also wild and unpredictable.

## SAND ART

On K'Gari, explorers can find 72 different colours of rainbow sand in reds, browns and yellows. Iron changes the colour of each sand grain, to make beautiful patterns across the dunes. Look from a distance – climbing on the sand collapses the beautiful rainbow.

## BUTCHULLA PEOPLE

The traditional owners of K'Gari understood the seasons and species of their home, so they could live in harmony with it. Scientists are working with Butchulla people to find special places on the island where spiritual and cultural events happened, so they can protect them as we learn more about these amazing people.

Each Butchulla person was given a totem – a symbol of a special animal and it was (and is) their job to protect that totem by not hunting, harming or eating it. This was sustainable living long ago and allowed all animals, plants and humans to live in perfect balance.

## FEATHER-TAILED GLIDER

Whoosh ... fur zooms above your head at night. This cheeky fellow appears to 'fly' between trees, feasting on delicious insects and nectar. A thin flap of skin (membrane) connects from their elbow to knee and makes them super fast gliders as they jump out of the branches. Trace down to their tail to find stiff barbs that make the shape look a little like a feather. Feathertails can glide up to 20m in one go. Compare your skills. How far can you jump?

## COOLOOLA SEDGE FROG

The Cooloola Sedge Frog is a special type of acid frog and loves K'Gari freshwater lakes because they have a very low pH. Acid frogs are tiny, rare and only live in this region – nowhere else. They have spent many years adapting to their special lake homes. They camouflage into reeds with their smooth green skin and munch on flies, spiders and moths.

## SHIPWRECKS

The ocean surrounding K'Gari is wild and dangerous and many ships have been wrecked along its shores. You can still see one today – the SS *Maheno*. It smashed its way to the shore in 1935 when a cyclone blew it off course. It's sharp and rusty, so use caution explorers.

## HUMPBACK WHALE

K'Gari is one of the best spots to wave to the locals as they swim by, migrating from south to north and back again. Humpback Whales sing their dreamy songs in these waters from July to November and have made a huge comeback from the brink of extinction years ago. These big grey babies grow up to 16 metres long! That's about 84 pencils or 4.5 small cars! Whales love to show off as they travel the coastline. Use the chart over the page to record how many behaviours you can spot. Don't forget to wave back.

# ACTIVITIES

## WICKED WHALES

Use the word search to discover ways whales communicate with their bodies.

TAIL SLAP
BLOW
CALF
HEAD SLAP
BREACH

```
C S B A L E E N B F
H U M P B A C K R Q
H C T X E C B F E C
S E M A P C J I A A
I I A I I P S N C L
C T N D G L S L H F
X J Y G S R S R A D
B L O W U L A L P P
R J Z I Y P A T A B
Y R D I V E L P E P
```

DIVE
HUMPBACK
SING
BALEEN
PEC SLAP
MIGRATE
FIN

## RANGER'S TIPS

Remember that the animals here are cute, but still wild and potentially dangerous.

During your visit, always do these things to stay Dingo safe:

- Walk with others
- Look from afar
- Keep food and rubbish sealed
- Never feed Dingoes

## TRY A TOTEM

Which animal is most special to you?

Design a symbol that represents the animal and how you will protect it.

## SAND SKETCHING

WHEN VISITING THE COLOURED CLIFFS, SIT QUIETLY WITH YOUR SKETCHBOOK AND DRAW THE AMAZING LINES AND COLOURS YOU SEE BEFORE YOU. A PERMANENT, PEACEFUL MEMORY TO TAKE HOME AND KEEP FOREVER.

# CARNARVON
## NATIONAL PARK

Welcome to a world of towering sandstone cliffs, where the river bends and twists. The water never stops flowing in beautiful Carnarvon Gorge and there are ancient artworks and hidden treasures to be found.

Get your boots on explorers!

# CARNARVON NATIONAL PARK
## ID CARD

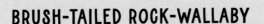

**PARK ESTABLISHED:** 1932
**KNOWN FOR:** Oasis on the plains
**SIZE:** 263km$^2$
**HOME OF:** Bidjara and Karingbal people
**GEOGRAPHY:** Sandstone cliffs, caves and gorges

LITTLE EXPLORER'S GUIDE

## BRUSH-TAILED ROCK-WALLABY

These shy, agile hoppers are listed as vulnerable in Queensland, which means we need to take extra care to protect them, so they don't become extinct.

Wallabies can all start to look the same after a while, but these special guys have a very long, bushy tail for balancing, strong legs for jumping and a white stripe along their cheek. They use their rough feet to stand and jump firmly on the rocks without slipping. They like to chill in rock caves and cracks during the day and peek out to search for grasses and fruits at dusk.

## FRESHWATER CATFISH

Fossicking just below the surface of the clear, fresh water, long sensitive whiskers feel for food. Catfish have slippery, slimy skin and eat algae and invertebrates on the riverbed.

## POWERFUL OWL

Peering through the darkness glow yellow eyes, atop a tall body, feathered legs and powerful, sharp talons. This is the largest owl in the country and is often found near waterways, where pairs mate for life in their own special territory. Listen for a low *woo-hoo* in the treetops at night because these owls live in small family groups and hunt for midnight treats of possums, gliders and birds. We must find a way to live in harmony with these magnificent birds as cars, habitat destruction and introduced species like foxes are dangerous for our owls.

## YELLOW-BELLIED GLIDER

By day, search for clues of these hungry furry friends, by checking eucalyptus for V-shaped cuts. Gliders save energy by leaping over 100m and slicing the bark of trees into a V, perfect for lapping up the sweet, sticky sap that oozes out from beneath. Yellow-bellieds are chatty and like to call to their mates to tell intruders to leave. At night, listen for a shriek then a low rattle from your campground.

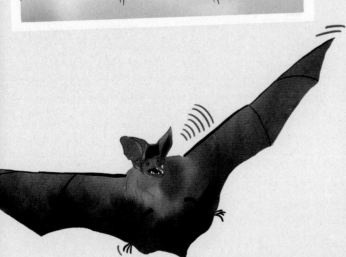

## RAINBOW BEE-EATER

Cheeky little Rainbows with curved beaks zip through the sky, catching insects on their way. When a bee-eater catches a bee, it uses its beak to rub the sting off against a tree before swallowing. Listen for their *prrp-prrp* calls and you might catch a glimpse of these colourful birds making tunnels for nests in the sandy banks.

## BATS

Carnarvon is a bat heaven. Twenty species live in this park and roost in trees and caves throughout. Bats need fresh water to drink, but cannot swim. This makes the gorge a perfect place for them to swoop down and take sips as they please. There are some cute-faced furry friends such as flying-foxes and some particularly strange-looking characters like the Gould's Long-eared Bat and the Little Bent-winged Bat. Carnarvon welcomes all sorts!

## CARNARVON CULTURE

The Bidjara and Karingbal people of this area tell the dreaming story of the rainbow serpent who carved out the gorge as it swam in and out of the creek with its huge, powerful body. Long before pen and paper, important messages and stories were recorded on cave walls. Take a walk along the Main Gorge Track to the 'Art Gallery' to uncover 2,000 pieces of ancient art that will take your breath away.

## WATTLE TREE

The Aboriginal people of this area have been shopping this 'natural supermarket' for thousands of years. Bread can be made by grinding wattle seeds into fine powder, mixing with water to make dough and placing into the ashes to bake. When the wattle flowers yellow, this tells you the time of year that fish are running.

# ACTIVITIES

## ROCK RECORDS

If you had to 'write a message' to the next person visiting Carnarvon to tell them all about your amazing trip, but you could only use pictures, what would it look like?

## ROCKING RAFTS

Collect some natural materials from your campground and see if you can make a raft that really floats.

1. Sketch out a design for your raft.
2. Collect bush materials that float or blow in the wind.
3. Assemble your raft.
4. Test it out.
5. What did you notice? Make changes as you go to improve your design or help it float.

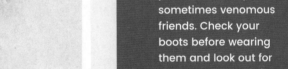
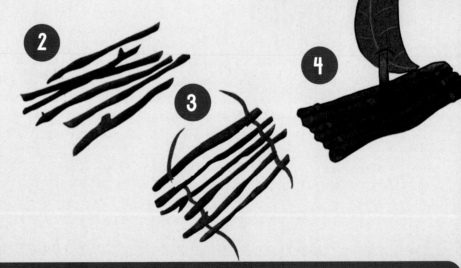

## RANGER'S TIPS

- **Hydrate to dominate:** Long walks sure use a lot of energy and our bodies need plenty of water to stay healthy. Pack plenty of water to get you through your adventures.

- **Be snake safe:** We share this beautiful national park with slithery and sometimes venomous friends. Check your boots before wearing them and look out for scales and sounds in long grass, open sunny areas and exposed rocks. Appreciate sleepy snakes from a distance, they deserve to enjoy the quiet too.

## SOUNDS OF THE BUSH

LISTEN TO NATURE AS YOU HIKE THROUGH THE GORGE AND AROUND YOUR CAMPSITE AT NIGHT. WHAT CAN YOU HEAR?

Record the sounds here and check back with your book later to find out what they were. For example, *prrrrp*.

# Diamantina
## NATIONAL PARK

In 1992, the Queensland Government turned these cattle stations into a national park to protect some of the most unique and vulnerable species in our country.

Drive across pale sandy plains, taking in massive blue skies to the quiet, wild lands of Diamantina. As the bush dries and floods, habitats and animal behaviour change, making every day different.

# DIAMANTINA NATIONAL PARK
## ID CARD

**PARK ESTABLISHED:** 1992
**KNOWN FOR:** Desert landscapes and water holes
**SIZE:** 5,070km²
**HOME OF:** Maiawali and Karuwali people
**GEOGRAPHY:** Sandstone ranges and floodplains

## LOVELY LAKES

Diamantina is one of the most important sites for migratory waterbirds and other species in Australia because it's so large and undisturbed. Ducks, swans, cuckoos, rails, egrets, plovers, godwits, sandpipers, stints, greenshanks, quails, gulls, terns, owls, kites, buzzards, eagles, falcons, parrots, fairy-wrens, honeyeaters and orioles are just a few birds you can see here! In fact, it's so rich in life that scientists are still discovering all the species that visit. Some birds migrate from the Northern Hemisphere all the way here (and back again) to chase the warm weather, travelling up to 10,000km each way for some species!

## KOWARI

These ultra-fast runners hold their tails at 90 degrees as they dash over the sand. Keep a look out for the black brush at the tip. Kowaris hide in burrows during the day and use their long whiskers to feel in the dark when they come out at night to feast on insects and carrion (dead things). Scientists have been using thermal imaging cameras that detect heat to track these super-speedy night runners.

## GREATER BILBY

Deep in the earth, down a spiral-shaped burrow, hide nocturnal creatures the size of a bunny, with giant ears and silky fur. Bilbies are specially designed for the outback – big ears for excellent hearing, feeding at night when it's cool and getting most of their water requirements from food alone. They used to live across the whole country, but seeing as they're the perfect size for feral cats to eat for dinner, with no way to protect themselves, our poor bilbies can now only be found in a few special places.

## NIGHT PARROT

Whistle… Whistle… No, it's not Uncle Kevin in the back paddock. You may just be in the presence of true mystery. The Night Parrot was thought to be extinct for 75 years, then seen again in 2013. Night Parrots are terrible fliers, so live on the ground where they come out at night to eat grass seeds. These parrots have been so hard to find because they have amazing camouflage, are nomadic and lay their eggs at the end of small tunnels amongst the spinifex. Now they've been rediscovered, scientists are working long and hard to protect their habitat and learn more about these strange fellows.

## INLAND TAIPAN

Taipans live all across Australia, but are well suited to the outback. They wait till big rains come, which causes rats to breed and then they have their own babies who eat the rats when they hatch – it's the perfect food web. Taipans are one of the deadliest species in the world with long fangs and plenty of venom. They like to hide underneath logs, rocks and plants. Be alert, explorers, but not alarmed!

## CRIMSON TURKEY BUSH

From March to October bold red flowers emerge from the bush, showing off petals in a peculiar tube shape. The flowers and leaves were traditionally crushed and rubbed on skin to work as a natural insect repellent.

## MAIAWALI AND KARUWALI TRADE ROUTE

Long ago, the Maiawali and Karuwali people followed the rain and traded information, culture and new technology along the Diamantina river. People sharing information sang songs and held ceremonies that gave great survival tips and helped them understand the world around them better; these are called 'song lines'. Some groups travelled up to 800km across country to reach the trade route here and looked at the stars to guide them at night.

# ACTIVITIES

## PEEKING PARROTS

How many Night Parrots can you spot in the picture with their amazing camouflage?

## KOWARI CHAOS

Work through the maze to find your way safely to the burrow. Watch out for threats along the way!

### RANGER'S TIPS

Scientists are working really hard to protect the bilbies and have even built a long fence in Queensland to keep cats out. To help them with their research, report bilby sightings to the Queensland Government.

During the wet season, floods can come out of nowhere. Check national park websites and local weather stations for weather alerts and notifications of track closures. Never drive or walk through flood waters.

**NIGHT SHOW**  *DRAW YOUR OWN 'MAP' OF THE NIGHT SKY IN YOUR NOTEBOOK.*

# EUNGELLA
## NATIONAL PARK

High in the clouds lie the 'mountains of the mist' –
Eungella in Aboriginal language. In the traditional
land of the Yuwibara, Widi and Barada Barna people
you can discover secret rainforest with views that
sweep across the land as far as the eye can see.
Beneath the bubbling rapids, hide elusive friends
fossicking the river depths for dinner.

# EUNGELLA NATIONAL PARK
## ID CARD

LITTLE EXPLORER'S GUIDE

**PARK ESTABLISHED:** 1936
**KNOWN FOR:** Expansive rivers and Platypus
**SIZE:** 529km²
**HOME OF:** Yuwibara, Widi and Barada Barna people
**GEOGRAPHY:** Steep mountains and deep gorges

## RED SOIL

Every plant and animal in this special place relies on the ancient rich, red soil to thrive. The base of the mountains are made of a hard rock called 'granite' that is tough and doesn't erode. On top lays a thick bed of deep soil, turned red by the iron and aluminium oxides that also make the soil full of nutrients needed to grow rainforest.

## PLATYPUS

As you peer into the dark, cool water, past your own reflection, watch carefully for bubbles floating to the surface. Platypus use special sensors in their bills to track the electrical signals of their prey underwater. They use their bills to forage and sift for invertebrates at the bottom which make the bubbles you can see. Then they stash the food in their cheeks to grind up later.

These monotremes are mammals, but unusually they lay eggs. Scientists initially found them so weird that they considered them to be a hoax. Platypus don't have pouches, so the mums curl up with the eggs to keep them warm in long burrows in the banks of the river.

## NOISY PITTA

Take a deep breath... what does it smell like? Did you know that Noisy Pittas have a sense of smell, unlike most other birds? In fact they love smelling so much that they build dome-shaped nests in beds of moist dung on the ground. These little fellas are so clever they can use tools like rocks or wood to smash open snail shells and eat the insides. Look out for broken shells and polished rocks as proof they've been around.

## KREFFT'S TURTLE

Many turtles live here, but can you spot the Krefft's? It likes to bask on logs and rocks in the sunshine and shelter under fallen trees in rivers. The babies only eat meat, but grow to love their veggies as they get older and become omnivorous. During droughts, Krefft's like to go on adventures to find water, so watch out for them crossing the road!

## EUNGELLA HONEYEATER

This special bird was mistaken for another widespread species of honeyeater until 1975, when scientists looked a little harder and realised it was in fact a new species. These fluttering beauties only live in this small patch of rainforest and spend their days in search of crystallised honeydew on Forest Red Gums. Listen for sharp, frantic whistles where plants are flowering.

## TAWNY FROGMOUTH

Everywhere around you are creatures great and small, this one so well camouflaged, you may not notice him at all! Tawny feathers perfectly match the colours of the trees in which they roost and since they can stay perfectly still, they're hard to spot. They have special feathers with soft edges that make no sound as they hunt at night for sneaking up on prey. Big eyes give frogmouths excellent vision at night and they use their wide, bright yellow mouth to make a soft *oom oom* sound.

## EUNGELLA DAY FROG

Take a trip down the range to explore the special rock called basalt at Finch-Hatton Gorge. This rock is softer than granite, so can be carved easily by water and here you'll find deep pools and crevices perfect for exploring. Keep your eyes peeled as you rockhop, for tiny chocolate brown frogs with a round nose and an 'x' mark on their back. These are the endangered Eungella Day Frogs. These guys like to hang out in the steep sections with splash zones and flick their legs and bob their heads to communicate.

## GREATER GLIDER

These big guys look like teddy bears and are sometimes called the 'clumsy cousins' as their skin membrane which allows them to glide is attached to their elbow, not their wrist. This makes it trickier to land, but funny to watch. They sleep in hollows during the day and perform glides of up to 100m at night, marking trees with their scent as they go. Explore with a torch at night and look way up high to get a lucky glimpse.

# ACTIVITIES

## SYMMETRY SKETCH

Use the grid to help you draw the other half of the Eungella Day Frog.

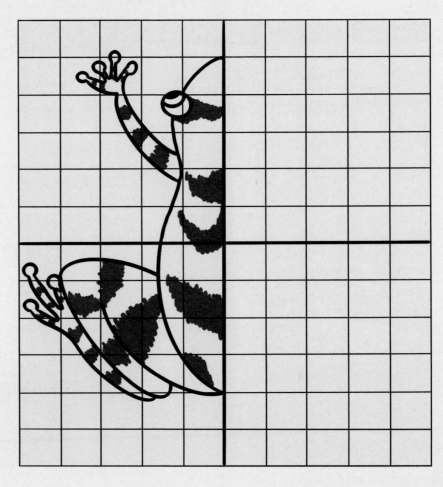

## EGG HUNT

Match the animal to the eggs – who doesn't belong?

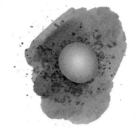

PLATYPUS

NOISY PITTA

TAWNY FROGMOUTH

GREATER GLIDER

ECHIDNA

## RANGER'S TIPS

Riverbeds and gorges can be slippery and unsafe. Excited explorers have met their peril in beautiful, wild places like this.

Always wear sturdy shoes and follow the advice on the signs which tell you where you can go and how to follow park rules.

## DIVE TIMES

COUNT THE TURTLES AND PLATYPUS DOWN BY BROKEN RIVER. TIME HOW LONG BETWEEN BUBBLING TO SURFACING AND COMPARE WHO CAN HOLD THEIR BREATH LONGER.

# Whitsunday
## ISLANDS NATIONAL PARK

Close your eyes and imagine the most beautiful tropical
island with crisp white sand and sapphire blue water.
Now multiply that by 74 ... welcome to the Whitsundays!

A magical new world awaits you here – just dip your
head underwater to discover it.

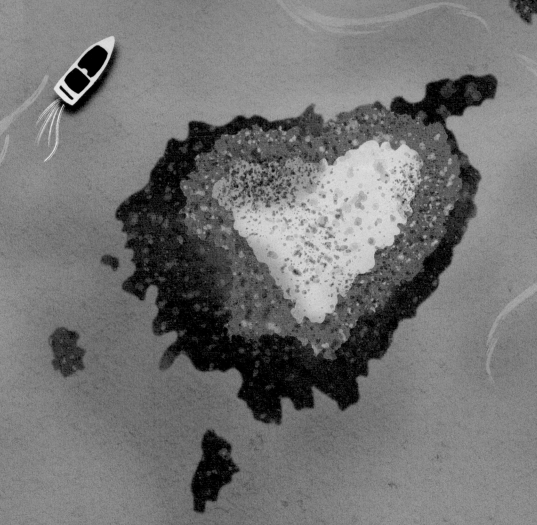

# WHITSUNDAY ISLANDS
# NATIONAL PARK ID CARD

**PARK ESTABLISHED:** Late 1930s
**KNOWN FOR:** Great Barrier Reef
**SIZE:** 170km²
**HOME OF:** Ngaro people
**GEOGRAPHY:** Chain of tropical islands

LITTLE EXPLORER'S GUIDE

## FAWN-FOOTED MELOMYS

Under the cover of night, little furry melomys forage for food. Long tails are used to wrap and balance (like possums) and instead of hair these tails have tiny scales. During the day, melomys make nests with leaves or in hollows and sleep hidden away from predators.

## CORAL REEFS

The Whitsunday islands lie on the edge of the worlds largest reef, The Great Barrier Reef. It's actually made up of over 3,000 individual reefs and is the only living thing you can see from space! Scientists believe the reef is around 20 million years old and there are over 400 different types of coral here. Corals are actually tiny animals called 'polyps' and thousands (or more) of them group together to make the pretty shapes you see underwater. Each year after a full moon, a mass spawning event occurs where the coral put out huge clouds of white across the ocean at night, to make new coral. The coral larva then need to find a clear space to attach and grow. Inside the bodies of coral live algae that make the colour we see. This algae is sensitive to high temperatures and pollution, so as these things increase in our oceans, it causes 'coral bleaching' and the algae dies. Ask your adults to help you research ways we can all reduce our environmental footprint and reduce global warming.

## WHITSUNDAY BOTTLE TREE

These chunky trees are only found on steep, low slopes around Proserpine in the Whitsundays – nowhere else in world. They flower in October and November and create seed pods shaped like little boats.. can you guess why? Their round shape is created from the water they store inside their trunks, just like a real bottle.

## JEWEL SPIDERS

As you wander about near creeks and wetlands, look out for jewel spiders, which are sometimes called 'spiny spiders'. Each one is small at just 1cm across, but they live in massive groups, sometimes with thousands of webs connected to each other! They make a web in the shape of a wheel and have six tough spines on their backs to stop insects and birds eating them. Look, but don't touch.

## GREEN SEA TURTLE

These huge, beautiful specimens weigh up to 150kg and are actually named after their green fat, not the colour of their shell or bodies. Parents lay eggs in the sand at 18 main nesting sites along the Great Barrier Reef. Sadly, climate change is causing the sand to become too hot, increasing beach erosion, washing away nests and raising the tide. All of these things make it hard for turtle babies and eggs to survive. We can all play our part keeping turtles safe from human impacts by doing things such as always driving slowly in boats, reporting sick or dead turtles and always placing rubbish in the bin.

## WHITE-BELLIED SEA EAGLE

With a short, square tail and distinctive honking call, these eagles are easy to spot. Their eyesight is twice as good as that of humans, with eyes further forward in their head (like binoculars) to allow them to zoom in really close.

Sea eagles can't break down all the parts of their prey in their bellies, so they regurgitate some of it and scientists use this information in research.

## NGARO PEOPLE

The traditional owners of this land believe the rainbow serpent slithered up the coast and carved out the way as she went, laying her eggs (islands) behind her. The Ngaro were some of the first people Captain Cook came across as the ship *Endeavour* sailed past their fishing boats. You can enjoy Ngaro rock art by visiting Hook Island.

## PROSERPINE ROCK-WALLABY

This shy, nocturnal mammal wasn't discovered until 1976 and can only be found near the town of Proserpine and on some Whitsunday Islands. It has the smallest range of any wallaby species. These marsupials have all-black paws and nails like hooks for expertly climbing over rocks and boulders where they shelter. Unfortunately land clearing, toxic weeds, feral animals, cars and diseases have all caused this sensitive species to become endangered. You may spot small groups of wallabies sharing rock piles or eating grass on the forest edge – keep quiet and still and enjoy the special moment.

# ACTIVITIES

## RAINBOW SERPENT

Colour each scale carefully to create your version of the rainbow serpent.

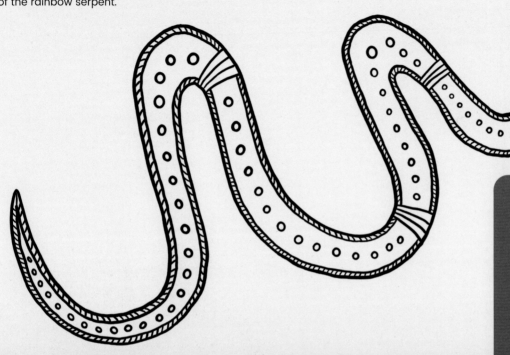

## RANGER'S TIPS

- **Be reef safe:** When out on the reef, look with your eyes, not your hands. The reef is fragile and we can enjoy it without breaking it.

- **Jellyfish:** You can enjoy the reef all year, but you'll need to wear a fancy-looking stinger suit from October to May.

## HISTORY UNCOVERED

Follow the wiggly lines to discover what the Ngaro people used each of these resources for:

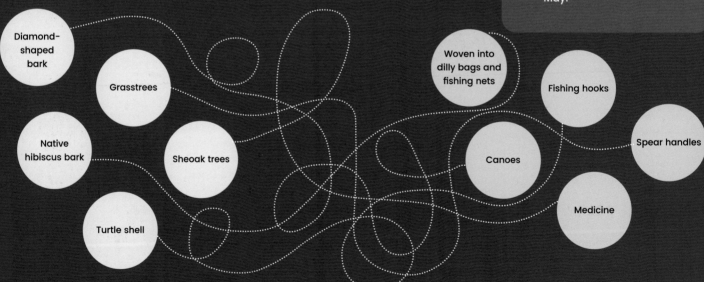

Diamond-shaped bark

Grasstrees

Native hibiscus bark

Sheoak trees

Turtle shell

Woven into dilly bags and fishing nets

Fishing hooks

Spear handles

Canoes

Medicine

## TIME CHALLENGE

TINY PIECES OF RUBBISH ALONG THE BEACH WASH INTO THE OCEAN AND HARM MARINE WILDLIFE. HOW MANY PIECES CAN YOU COLLECT IN 5 MINUTES?

Discuss with your family some ways you could reduce your waste at home and school to have an even bigger impact.

# DAINTREE
## NATIONAL PARK

Sunlight streams through the canopy, flickering in warm gold and fresh green. Things are just bigger here – treetops as tall as skyscrapers, cunning prehistoric reptiles and giant birds that make tents look tiny.

In the Daintree you can experience the past, present and future all in a day as you marvel at animals and plants from long ago, experience fun in the moment and commit to a better future for special places like this.

## DAINTREE NATIONAL PARK
### ID CARD

PARK ESTABLISHED: 1988
KNOWN FOR: Prehistoric animals and plants
SIZE: 1,200km²
HOME OF: Kuku Yalanji Bubu people
GEOGRAPHY: Rainforest by the sea

### ULYSSES BUTTERFLY

The Ulysses flies fast to escape predators – it looks like an electric blue flash through the leaves. They have tiny overlapping scales on their wings, which gives them their colour. As butterflies gather nectar, they pollinate flowers.

### SOUTHERN CASSOWARY

Stomp, stomp – giant powerful legs tipped with three long, strong claws march their way through the rainforest. These flightless, endangered birds can run at speeds of up to 50km per hour and tower to 2 metres tall. Their head is topped with a brown helmet called a 'casque'. Look for clues on your travels like listening for 'grunts' through the forest, dung piles filled with seeds or large three-toed footprints.

Cassowary are incredibly important to their habitat, because their favourite thing to eat is rainforest fruits and their waste helps to disperse the seed and make new baby plants, keeping the forest alive.

### INDIGENOUS LANGUAGE

The Eastern Kuku Yalanji Bubu, the local Aboriginal people, lived here for over 9,000 years before invasion. They lived with the animals and plants to ensure species were protected and they could get the food, shelter and medicine they needed.

Some of the language has been saved.
Here are some common words:

Bana – fresh water
Bayan – house
Jalun – sea
Karrangkal – coral reef
Kurranji – cassowary

Madja – rainforest
Mungurru – mangrove
Ngawiya – turtle
Jarba – snake

JALUN
KURRANJI
BAYAN
NGAWIYA

### WATERFALL FROG

Waterfall Frogs became endangered in 2000 because they must live near fast-flowing water and have been dying from a fungus that affects their delicate skin. They love hanging out on rocks in waterfalls and streams and use their strong sucking mouths to 'hold on' so they don't get swept away.

# AMETHYSTINE PYTHON

Slippery and smooth, Amethystine Pythons can't break their food with their teeth, so they have to swallow everything whole, even animals as large as a wild pig! They 'listen' to vibrations with their bodies and use their tongue to 'smell' food.

They grow at least 7 metres long and are the biggest snake in Australia. Mum stays with the eggs until they hatch and she twitches her body to create extra heat to keep them comfortable.

# BENNETT'S TREE-KANGAROO

High in the canopy, furry mammals with muscly legs leap between trees. They are secretive as they rest during the day and emerge to eat leaves and fruits at night. It's no wonder they evolved from the ancestors of possums.

Like hairy bouncy balls, tree-kangaroos can jump down 30 metres but keep a watchful eye for dingoes and pythons who would like to catch them for dinner.

# ANCIENT TREES

The Daintree is the largest rainforest in Australia and the oldest rainforest in the world at around 180 million years old.

# BOYD'S FOREST DRAGON

Find this lizard hanging on to tree trunks in patches of sun after rain. Their triangle-shaped head with a spiny crest on top makes them look like a real baby dinosaur. Boyd's move slowly and so need very good camouflage. It's important to keep researching these lizards because we still don't know much about their habitat.

# INSECTS

We still haven't discovered all the insects in the Daintree yet, but scientists estimate there are around 12,000 different species. Insects are so important for eating leaves and breaking down wood to make new soil and habitats for other animals. Take a photo – I wonder if you'll discover something new?

# SALTWATER CROCODILE

Sailing just below the surface of the Daintree river, you will find a scaly beast almost unchanged in 240 million years. This former companion of the dinosaurs is perfectly adapted to its tropical home, and it's the biggest reptile in the world!

'Salties' make a compost mound and lay special eggs that don't dry out. Everything has a place in the food chain and croc eggs and hatchlings are taken by lizards, fish, sharks and birds. No wonder croc parents are so fierce.

Crocodiles have a flap of skin to block their throat while swimming so they can breathe underwater and sneak up on prey. They can even swim almost 1,000km in one go without food … that's Brisbane to Sydney!

# ACTIVITIES

## FIND MY FOOD

Recheck your animal facts on the previous page to find out who eats what.
Draw an arrow from the animal to the food it likes to eat and discover the complex food web of the rainforest.

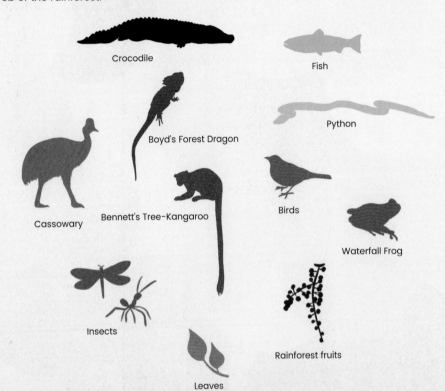

Crocodile

Fish

Boyd's Forest Dragon

Python

Cassowary

Bennett's Tree-Kangaroo

Birds

Waterfall Frog

Insects

Rainforest fruits

Leaves

1m

1m

## RAINFOREST MATHS

1. Find an open patch of rainforest near your campsite and draw a square on the ground with a stick. Scientists call this a 'quadrat'. Your square should be about 1m by 1m.
2. Get down low, turn over some leaves and soil and count how many insects you can find inside your square.
3. Times your insect number by 1,000,000 to find out how many insects are in a square kilometre.

For example, 35 insects x 1,000,000 = 35,000,000 insects for every square **kilometre** of forest.

AMETHYSTINE PYTHONS GROW TO 7 METRES. ASK AN ADULT TO HELP YOU PACE OUT THEIR LENGTH AND USE A STICK TO DRAW AN OUTLINE IN THE SAND OR SOIL. DECORATE WITH ROCKS, TWIGS AND LEAVES FOR EVEN MORE FUN.

# BOODJAMULLA
## NATIONAL PARK

Hidden among the vast plains where the desert seems to go on forever, is a secret oasis we call Boodjamulla National Park. Rocky red paths lead to enormous towering cliffs, plunging into deep, blue, cool fresh water.

Are you ready for a wild ride?

## BOODJAMULLA NATIONAL PARK
### ID CARD

**PARK ESTABLISHED:** 1984
**KNOWN FOR:** Dinosaur fossils
**SIZE:** 2,820km²
**HOME OF:** Waanyi people
**GEOGRAPHY:** Ancient sandstone on grassy plains

## RIVERSLEIGH FOSSILS

In the south-east corner of the park, you can explore the very special World Heritage Area of Riversleigh. Imagine travelling back in time 40 million years, to when Gondwana broke into its parts, creating Australia and other continents.

The animals living on our land evolved into their own special species and you can find over 250 fossil sites right here. Maybe you'll see a Fangaroo (small kangaroo with giant canine teeth) or a Mekosuchus (goanna crocodile that climbed trees). I wonder what you'll learn about the future by looking into the past?

## OLIVE PYTHON

The second-largest snake in Australia weighs over 40kg and hunts food as big as wallabies at night. Olives are extremely powerful and they use constriction (squeezing) rather than venom to kill their prey. They like to hide out in rocky sections, inside caves or hollow logs, but are also amazing swimmers. Olive Pythons have the most beautiful smooth skin – it looks this way because they have lots of small scales very close together across their bodies.

## GULF SNAPPING TURTLE

Science is tricky and sometimes it takes a few goes to get it right. In 1997, scientists discovered a turtle in this park that looked the same as the fossils from the area. Of course, they thought it might be a living descendant of the fossil turtle they thought was extinct. However, 23 years later in 2020, they could gather more information and realised this living turtle was actually a new species. This turtle is endangered and we're still learning about it. The top of its head has a thick, horny shield – what do you think it's used for?

## PURPLE-CROWNED FAIRY-WREN

With only 7,000 left in the wild, this high-energy feathered friend is special to see. During the breeding season, males wear a beautiful purple crown to attract a mate. Look out for these fairy-wrens near rivers. They live in tight family groups and all family members pitch in to feed babies and ward off predators. Even the older brothers and sisters stay back to help raise new siblings – talk about teamwork.

## ROCK RING-TAILED POSSUM

Not just any possums, scientists have observed them cuddling their babies for fun and comfort – no other animals have been seen to do this except apes.

Rock Ring-taileds live in the cliffs and you can see them walking in single file, making 'body bridges' between rocks. They do a great job of spreading fruit and blossom seeds through their scats (poo) and sometimes smack their tails on rocks to communicate.

## WAANYI WEATHER

For many thousands of years, the Waanyi have used expert observation skills to notice changes in the plants and animals to help them predict the weather. Each part of the environment has a special story for the Waanyi people and all are connected to each other.

RAINBOW    CLOUD    RAIN    SUN

## FRESHWATER CROCODILE

Skinny noses and needle-sharp teeth make these crocs seem tiny compared to 'Salties'. 'Freshies' in this park move to different areas as the rivers flood and dry, and shelter in burrows under tree roots during the day. They are 'pulse nesters' – all the crocodiles lay eggs around the same time and the babies hatch at the start of the wet season. If threatened, the parents will puff up their bodies, shudder, open their mouths and ... growl!

# ACTIVITIES

## VERY VENN

Use the Venn diagram circles to record which species live on land, which only in water and those that can do both!

LAND

WATER

BOTH

## RANGER'S TIPS

**Time your adventures** – clever science explorers use their knowledge of the animals and plants of the area to time when to visit or explore.

You might like to think about the time of day, time of year, favourite foods, hiding places or relaxing places of the species you are looking for, to help you find them.

Have your binoculars, camera and sketchbook ready!

## SPOT THE DIFFERENCE

Compare the two crocodiles. How many differences can you find? In this activity you need to focus on tiny details, just like scientists do when spotting and describing new species.

## NATURE PORTRAIT

USE NATURAL MATERIALS AROUND YOUR CAMPGROUND TO DESIGN A PORTRAIT OF YOURSELF OR A FRIEND IN THE SOIL.

# FINAL QUIZ

Now that you've finished your reading and exploring, here's one last quiz to check what you learned. Check back through the book for the answers.

**1** Use the park ID cards to work out which is the oldest national park in the book.

**2** How many herbivores are listed in the book?

**3** What does 'monotreme' mean?

**4** Name three strange behaviours of different animals that they use when threatened.

**5** What was your favourite park to visit and why?

**6** What are four important things explorers should always do to keep our plants and animals safe when visiting national parks?

**7** List an animal that was thought to be extinct, but was then discovered alive at a Queensland national park.

**8** Tell us about a new friend you made on your travels (can be human or animal).

**9** What are four important things you should always pack ready for a day of exploring?

**10** How does it make you feel when you spend time outdoors in our beautiful national parks?

Answers on inside back cover.

## KEYWORDS EXPLAINED

| | |
|---|---|
| **Camouflage** | When animals and plants match their colours to their surroundings to blend in and hide from predators. |
| **Carnivore** | Eats only meat. |
| **Chrysalis** | The hard, protective shell that caterpillars use to rest inside as they transform into a butterfly. |
| **Colony** | A group of animals living together. |
| **Colonisation** | The time in history when explorers from other countries arrived in Australia and claimed the land as their own. |
| **Dung** | Animal poo. |
| **Ecologist** | A scientist who studies animals, plants, air and water. |
| **Extinct** | When all the animals and plants of a particular species has died out. |
| **Fauna** | Animals. |
| **Flora** | Plants. |
| **Habitat** | The place where animals and plants live and gain everything they require to survive. |
| **Herbivore** | Eats only plant matter. |
| **Hibernate** | When animals rest for long periods without eating or reproducing. |
| **Invertebrate** | Animals without backbones. |
| **Lichen** | A crusty-looking plant-like lifeform that covers trees and rocks. |

| | |
|---|---|
| **Macropod** | A family of marsupials that includes kangaroos and wallabies. |
| **Mammal** | Warm-blooded animals that produce milk. |
| **Marsupial** | A family of mammals that have pouches. |
| **Metamorphic** | The complete change of an animal from one thing to another in its life cycle. |
| **Migrate** | When animals temporarily move from one area to another in search of food, a mate or better weather. |
| **Monotreme** | A family of egg-laying mammals that includes echidnas and platypus. |
| **Nocturnal** | Animals that sleep during the day and hunt or forage at night. |
| **Nomadic** | Animals that travel and live in different places at different times. |
| **Omnivore** | Eats both meat and plant matter. |
| **Plumage** | Feathers. |
| **Predator** | An animal or plant that eats other animals or plants. |
| **Prey** | An animal or plants that gets eaten by other animals or plants. |
| **Roost** | When animals rest or sleep up high in trees or other structures. |
| **Talons** | Large, sharp claws. |

# PLEDGE TO THE PLANET

Now you know all about Queensland national parks and how to make better choices to protect plants, animals and culture, you can show your commitment by saying the pledge.

Have an adult record you speaking the pledge and signing it.

As a child of the world and a responsible citizen of our community,
I pledge to do what I can at home, at school and in my community,
To use less stuff,
Find new ways to do things,
Get outside more often,
Keep my distance from wild animals,
Respect and celebrate the culture of the places I visit,
Tell people about the amazing things I've learnt about nature; and
Do the right thing even when nobody is looking.
I love my planet and we can all work together to keep it healthy for our future.

Signed . . . . . . . . . . . . . . . . . . . . . . . . . . . . . . . . . . . . . . . . . . . . . .

## FIND OUT MORE

For keen little scientists wanting to read more about the fascinating animals, plants and culture detailed in this book, here are some suggestions:

**Queensland National Parks Service** parks.des.qld.gov.au
**Queensland Museum** www.qm.qld.gov.au
**Queensland State Archives** www.qld.gov.au/recreation/arts/heritage/archives

**State Library of Queensland** www.slq.qld.gov.au
**Australian Museum** australian.museum

Published in 2023 by Reed New Holland Publishers
Sydney

Level 1, 178 Fox Valley Road, Wahroonga, NSW 2076, Australia

newhollandpublishers.com

Copyright © 2023 Reed New Holland Publishers
Copyright © 2023 in text: Chloe Butterfield
Copyright © 2023 in illustrations: Deborah Bianchetto

Printed in China

10 9 8 7 6 5 4 3 2

A record of this book is held at the National Library of Australia.

ISBN 978 1 76079 521 4

Managing Director: Fiona Schultz
Publisher and Project Editor: Simon Papps
Production Director: Arlene Gippert

## OTHER TITLES BY REED NEW HOLLAND INCLUDE:

*Colour With Chris Humfrey's Awesome Australian Animals*  ISBN 978 1 76079 424 8
*Chris Humfrey's Awesome Australian Animals*  ISBN 978 1 92554 670 5

*Chris Humfrey's Coolest Creepy Crawlies*  ISBN 978 1 76079 445 3
*Colour With Chris Humfrey's Coolest Creepy Crawlies*  ISBN 978 1 76079 546 7

For details of hundreds of other Natural History titles see newhollandpublishers.com

And keep up with Reed New Holland and New Holland Publishers on Facebook and Instagram
 ReedNewHolland and NewHollandPublishers  @ReedNewHolland and @NewHollandPublishers